W9-CGR-239

ARSENAL
F.C.

BY

MARK STEWART

NORWOODHOUSE PRESS

Chicago, Illinois

NORWOODHOUSE PRESS

P.O. Box 316598 • Chicago, Illinois 60631
For more information about Norwood House Press please visit our website at
www.norwoodhousepress.com or call 866-565-2900.

Photography and Collectibles:
The trading cards and other memorabilia assembled in the background for this book's cover and interior pages
are all part of the author's collection and are reproduced for educational and artistic purposes.

All photos courtesy of Associated Press except the following individual photos and artifacts (page numbers):
Edizioni Panini (6), Gallaher Ltd. (10 top), Imperial Tobacco Co. (10 bottom), Topps, Inc. (11 top, 16),
World Soccer/IPC Media (11 middle), Hit HKF (11 bottom), Rafo/Mostar (22).

Cover image: Associated Press (Rex Features via AP Images)

Designer: Ron Jaffe
Series Editor: Mike Kennedy
Content Consultants: Michael Jacobsen and Jonathan Wentworth-Ping
Project Management: Black Book Partners, LLC
Editorial Production: Lisa Walsh

LIBRARY OF CONGRESS CATALOGING-IN-PUBLICATION DATA
Names: Stewart, Mark, 1960 July 7- author.
Title: Arsenal F.C. / By Mark Stewart.
Description: Chicago Illinois : Norwood House Press, 2017. | Series: First
   Touch Soccer | Includes bibliographical references and index. | Audience:
   Age 5-8. | Audience: K to Grade 3.
Identifiers: LCCN 2016058204 (print) | LCCN 2017005790 (ebook) | ISBN
   9781599538563 (library edition : alk. paper) | ISBN 9781684040759 (eBook)
Subjects: LCSH: Arsenal Football Club--History--Juvenile literature.
Classification: LCC GV943.6.A76 S84 2017 (print) | LCC GV943.6.A76 (ebook) |
   DDC 796.334/640941--dc23
LC record available at https://lccn.loc.gov/2016058204

302N--072017
Manufactured in the United States of America in North Mankato, Minnesota.

CONTENTS

Words in **bold type** are defined on page 24.

Mesut Ozil takes to the air against Southampton. Arsenal plays in the Premier League, England's top soccer league.

MEET ARSENAL F.C.

How would you like to be a goalkeeper facing a team called The Gunners? That is what fans of the Arsenal Football Club call their team. When people say "football" in England they are talking about soccer, not American football.

The Gunners live up to their nickname. They are always thinking of ways to create great shots for one another. This was true a century ago and it is still true today.

Arsenal started in the 1880s as a soccer club for workers at the royal arsenal in London. They made bullets, bombs, and cannonballs for the English army and navy. It was dangerous work. Soccer was a great way to relax. In the 1930s, Arsenal may have been the best team in the world. It went on to win more than a dozen league championships. The club's great players include **Cliff Bastin**, Tony Adams, David Seaman, and Ian Wright.

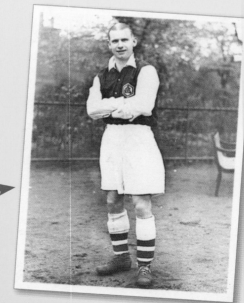

6

Ian Wright gets a double hug from teammates after scoring in a 2014 match.

The players may look tiny in this photo of Arsenal's new stadium, but it is still a wonderful place to watch a game.

8

BEST SEAT IN THE HOUSE

Arsenal played in a beautiful old stadium for more than 90 years. No matter how many changes the club made, fans wanted more. In 2006, Arsenal left to play in a brand new stadium about 15 minutes away. Since then, many clubs in England and Europe have copied its style. It is one of the best places in the country to watch soccer.

COLLECTOR'S CORNER

These collectibles show some of the best Arsenal players ever.

ALEX. JAMES

ALEX JAMES

Forward

1929–1937

James was the star of the great teams built by **manager** Herbert Chapman. Time and again, James set up teammates for easy goals.

TED DRAKE

Forward

1934–1945

Drake was a fearless attacker. He set a record with seven goals in one game.

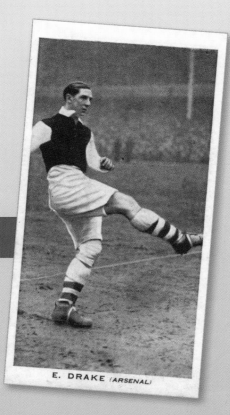

E. DRAKE (ARSENAL)

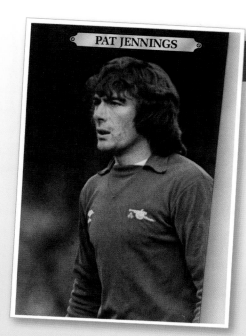

PAT JENNINGS

PAT JENNINGS

Goalkeeper
1977–1985
Some thought Jennings was "too old" at age 32 when he joined Arsenal. He led the club to three **FA Cup** finals in a row!

DENNIS BERGKAMP

Forward
1995–2006
Bergkamp was a nightmare for defenders. He seemed to come out of nowhere to make perfect passes or score spectacular goals.

World Cup Superstars
DENNIS BERGKAMP
Holland and Arsenal

WORLD SOCCER

THIERRY HENRY

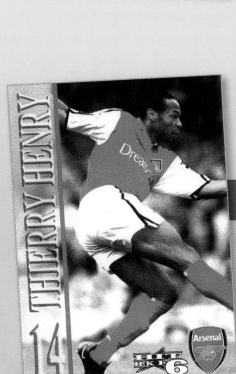

Forward
1999–2007
Henry was Arsenal's greatest one-on-one player. He helped the club play 49 matches in a row without losing in 2003 and 2004.

WORTHY OPPONENTS

London is a crowded city with many soccer clubs. Arsenal's main rivals play less than a half-hour away. Matches against Tottenham Hotspur are called the North London Derby. Games with Chelsea, Fulham, and West Ham United also draw large and noisy crowds.

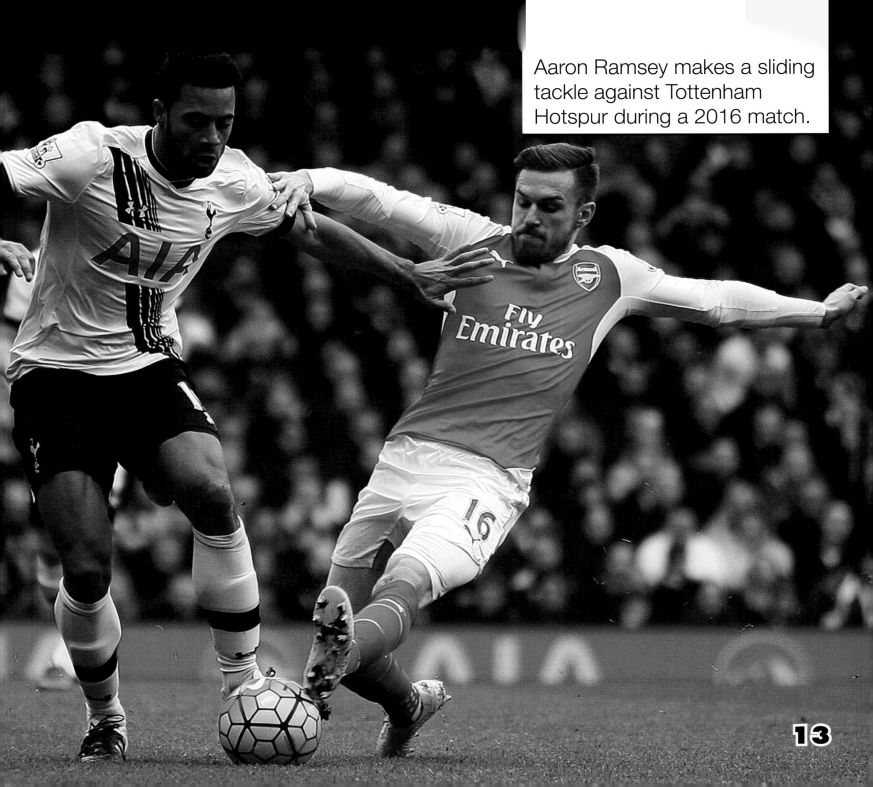

Aaron Ramsey makes a sliding tackle against Tottenham Hotspur during a 2016 match.

CLUB WAYS

Arsenal is known for having players from all over the world. That may be the reason why it has fans in over 100 countries. Nearly 100 million people follow the team on websites and social media. Arsenal plays in a part of London that is home to many different ethnic groups. Arsenal's fans are as diverse as its players.

Arsenal fans celebrate another victory by their Gunners.

15

ON THE MAP

Arsenal brings together players from many countries. These are some of the best:

1 **Tomas Rosicky** • Prague, Czech Republic

2 **Robert Pires** • Reims, France

3 **Robin van Persie** • Rotterdam, Netherlands

4 **Patrick Vieira** • Dakar, Senegal

5 **Kolo Toure** • Bouake, Ivory Coast

6 **Alexis Sanchez** • Tocopilla, Chile

7 **Gilberto Silva** • Lagoa da Prata, Brazil

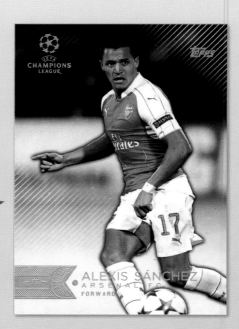

NORTH

WEST EAST

SOUTH

MAP OF EUROPE

Arsenal's home stadium is in London, England.

WORLD MAP

17

Arsenal's famous cannon crest is easy to see on the home uniform of Alexis Sanchez.

KIT AND CREST

Arsenal players have worn red and white shirts with white shorts for most of the club's history. The team's away kit changes often, but usually is a mix of yellow and blue. The club crest is a shield with a gold cannon. Although the crest has changed over the years, it has always included a cannon.

WE WON!

In English soccer, the aim of every team is to win a "double." To do this, a club must finish the season in first place and also win the FA Cup tournament. Arsenal did this for the first time in 1970–71. That season, the Gunners beat Tottenham Hotspur 1–0 to wrap up first place. Five days later, they met Liverpool in the FA Cup final. John Radford and Charlie George teamed up to score the winning goal in **extra time**. Arsenal won, 2–1.

Charlie George celebrates the goal that brought Arsenal its first "double," in 1971.

FOR THE RECORD

Arsenal has won more than 30 major championships!

Football League/ Premier League

13 championships
(from 1930–31 to 2003–04)

Cup Winners' Cup

1993–94

League Cup*

1965	2007
1998	2015
2005	

The League Cup is one of three annual tournaments held among English soccer clubs.

FA Cup

12 championships
(from 1929–30 to 2014–15)

Cesc Fabregas

CESC FABREGAS

These stars have won major awards while playing for Arsenal:

2001	Patrick Vieira • UEFA "Team of the Year" Midfielder
2001	Thierry Henry • UEFA "Team of the Year" Forward
2002	Thierry Henry • UEFA "Team of the Year" Forward
2003	Thierry Henry • UEFA "Team of the Year" Forward
2004	Thierry Henry • UEFA "Team of the Year" Forward
2004	Thierry Henry • Golden Shoe Award
2004	Ashley Cole • UEFA "Team of the Year" Defender
2005	Thierry Henry • Golden Shoe Award
2006	Thierry Henry • UEFA "Team of the Year" Forward
2006	Cesc Fabregas • UEFA "Team of the Year" Midfielder
2006	Jens Lehmann • Goalkeeper of the Year
2008	Cesc Fabregas • UEFA "Team of the Year" Midfielder
2013	Mesut Ozil • UEFA "Team of the Year" Midfielder

Soccer Words

Index

Extra Time
The two 15-minute periods played when a match is tied after 90 minutes.

FA Cup
The championship tournament of English soccer.

Manager
The person who runs a soccer team during games, like a basketball coach or baseball manager in the U.S.

Photos are on **BOLD** numbered pages.

About the Author

Mark Stewart has been writing about world soccer since the 1990s, including *Soccer: A History of the World's Most Popular Game*. In 2005, he co-authored Major League Soccer's 10-year anniversary book.

About Arsenal F.C.

Learn more at these websites:

www.arsenal.com/home

www.fifa.com

www.teamspiritextras.com